I RECOMMEND

A Complete Warm-Up Technique Book Designed to Improve Fundamental Musicianship

An ideal supplement to individual instruction, class lessons or full band rehearsals!

By JAMES D. PLOYHAR

with individual TUNING suggestions and WARM-UP exercises by Harold Brasch, William Bunch, Mervin Britton, Charles DeLaney, Larry Ford, Frederick Hemke, Lyle Merriman, Jack Rausch, Frank Stalzer, Paul Tanner and Stuart Uggen.

INSTRUMENTATION

CONDUCTOR	B♭ BASS CLARINET	TROMBONE
C FLUTE	E♭ ALTO SAXOPHONE	BARITONE BASS CLEF
OBOE	B♭ TENOR SAXOPHONE	BARITONE TREBLE CLEF
BASSOON	E♭ BARITONE SAXOPHONE	BASS (TUBA)
B♭ CLARINET	HORN IN F	DRUMS
E♭ ALTO CLARINET (E♭ Clarinet)	B♭ CORNET–TRUMPET	

TABLE OF CONTENTS

	Student Book	Conductor Book
UNIT I — Tuning-Warm Up (For Individual Use)	2	2
UNIT II — Lip Slurs (Brasses)	4	4
UNIT III — Chorales	5	6
UNIT IV — Major Scales and Scale Studies	7	11
UNIT V — Minor Scales	13	23
UNIT VI — Chromatic Scales	15	27
UNIT VII — Arpeggios	16	29
UNIT VIII — Interval Studies	17	31
UNIT IX — Articulation and Dynamic Studies — Staccato, Slur-Legato, Semi-Staccato, Tenuto, Accents and Dynamics	21	39
UNIT X — Rhythm Studies	24	42
UNIT XI — Rudiment Review	30	53

Unit I

TUNING - WARM UP
By William F. Bunch

For Bass or Tuba use only

INTONATION can be a considerable problem when a bass or tuba has only three valves and no convenient method of manipulating the individual valve slides (especially the first) while playing. On all tubas, the second harmonic notes on the fingerings 1-2-3, 1-3 and 1-2 are sharp. On many instruments the player has little recourse other than lipping the B and C down and playing the D with the third valve. The fourth valve offers alternate fingerings for the B and C which are more adequately in tune:

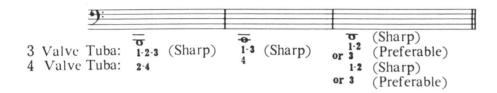

3 Valve Tuba: 1-2-3 (Sharp)   1-3 (Sharp)   or 1-2 / 3 (Sharp) / (Preferable)
4 Valve Tuba: 2-4   1-2 (Sharp) / or 3 (Preferable)

Dr. William F. Bunch
Performer, Clinician,
Assistant Professor and
Coordinator of Instrumental
Music and Low Brass Instructor,
Moorhead (Minn.) State College

The fourth valve provides an alternate fingering for any note fingered 1-3. When combined with the second valve it provides a substitute for 1-2-3. The fourth valve also makes it possible to play certain notes linking the fundamental with the second harmonic. These notes are not naturally available on the three valved instruments:

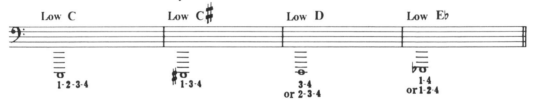

Low C   Low C#   Low D   Low Eb
1-2-3-4   1-3-4   3-4   1-4
                               or 2-3-4   or 1-2-4

Three-valved tubas with tuning slides that can be manipulated while playing can provide relatively good intonation if the following first valve slide adjustments are made:

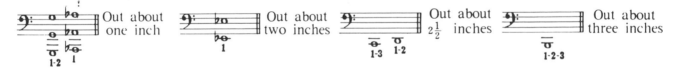

Out about one inch (1-2)   Out about two inches (1)   Out about 2½ inches (1-3 / 1-2)   Out about three inches (1-2-3)

These adjustments should **not** be considered absolute. Since individual instruments may vary they should be considered merely guidelines or approximations. The player must rely upon his own sense of pitch to make the adjustment best suited to his instrument.

GENERAL CONSIDERATIONS:

While playing, the throat and mouth cavities should be kept as open as possible. In articulating, the syllable "tah" will facilitate this openness. Continuous air support with projection **through** the horn is a must. This necessitates **deep breathing** . . . an intake of air considerably beyond that of normal inhalation. Large quantities of air must be obtained quickly through the mouth but in a relaxed manner similar to that of a yawn.

Care must be taken that the cheeks do not puff. A firmness at the corners of the mouth should help alleviate this problem. Since the cup of the tuba mouthpiece is quite large, the player must check against undue closure of the aperture between the teeth. The lower jaw must be free to drop and open more as the player descends into the lower register.

The warm-up exercises that follow are divided into two categories: 1) **Slurred Exercises** and 2) **Tongued Exercises.** These exercises progress from easy to moderately difficult.

Less advanced players should start with those exercises which they can perform easily, and gradually progress to the more difficult studies. More advanced players should perform the entire series of exercises **in sequence** as a daily routine.

A suggested warm-up routine for the less advanced player is as follows:

I.   Slurred Exercises #1, 2 and 6.   II.   Tongued Exercise #1.

It is recommended that all exercises be played initially at a slow speed. The player can gradually increase the tempo of the more advanced exercises as his flexibility and technique develop.

DAILY PRACTICE EXERCISES

I. Slurred Exercises:

II. Tongued Exercises:

It is suggested that this pattern be transposed to other major scales.

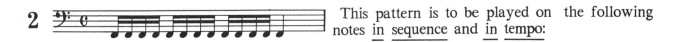

This pattern is to be repeated on each degree of the B♭ Major Scale

This pattern is to be played on the following notes in sequence and in tempo:

LIP SLURS (Brasses)

Although the following exercises are commonly called "lip slurs" it is the action of the tongue and the speed of the air stream that actually produces the slur. This can be demonstrated by whistling an interval of a fourth or a fifth. For a lower tone the back of the tongue assumes an "ah" or flatter position. For higher tones the back of the tongue assumes an "ee" or higher position. "Tah-ee" is used to slur from a low note to a higher note and "tee-ah" from a high note to a lower note.

CHORALES

Chorales are considered the best musical device for developing tone, balance, phrasing, breath support and intonation. The chorales are to be played in a slow, deliberate manner allowing each player sufficient time to <u>listen</u>! Each chorale is preceded by a tuning exercise in the appropriate key. The Roman numerals indicate the chord. The Arabic numerals next to the note indicate the note's position within the chord. Your director will instruct you as to how to balance the tuning chords.

Tuning

Break Forth, **O** Beauteous Heavenly Light

Sleepers, Awake

6

Tuning

Key of E♭ Major

5

Now Thank We All Our God

Johann Crüger (1598—1662)

6

Ⓐ

Tuning

Key of A♭ Major

7

Tallis' Canon

Thomas Tallis (1510—1585)

8

Tuning

Key of c Minor

9

O Sacred Head Now Wounded

H. L. Hassler (1564—1612)

10

Ⓐ   Ⓑ

MAJOR SCALES

Key of Bb Major

Scale Study

Key of Eb Major

Scale Study

10   Key of G♭ Major

Chords

Scale Study

Pares

Key of G Major

Chords

Scale Study
(Transposed-See #27)

Pares

MINOR SCALES

CHROMATIC SCALES

> Memorize your chromatic fingerings so that you can play an ascending and descending chromatic scale starting on any note.

Apply the following articulation patterns to the scales above: (Gradually increase speed!)

ARPEGGIOS

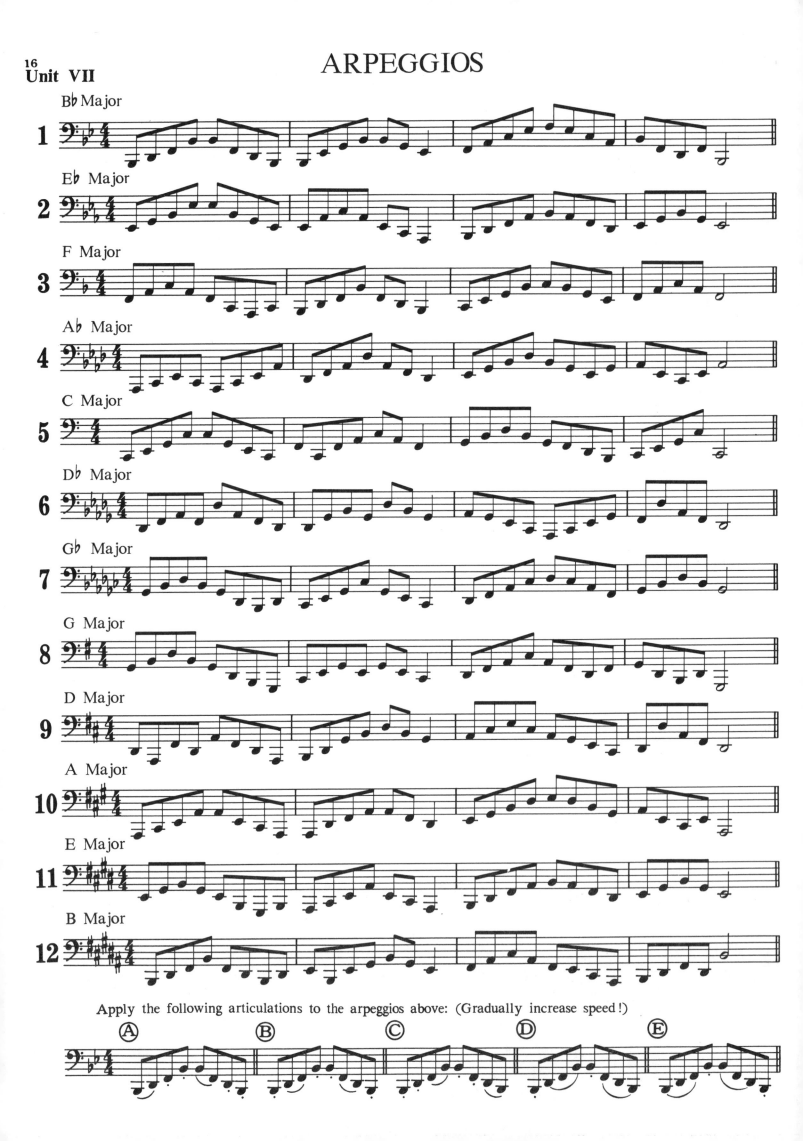

Apply the following articulations to the arpeggios above: (Gradually increase speed!)

INTERVAL STUDIES

Apply the following articulation patterns to the arpeggios in Unit VIII: (Gradually increase speed!)

ARTICULATION AND DYNAMIC STUDIES
Staccato

A dot (·) placed over or under a note calls for a crisp, detached STACCATO sound in which the length of the note is curtailed by at least one-half of its original value. A dash (▾) placed over or under a note indicates an ACCENTED STACCATO.

Apply the following to the B♭ (Major) Concert scale:

Staccato Etude

Slur-Legato

The SLUR or LEGATO indicates that all notes enclosed are to be played without any perceptible interruption. The tongue is used only to begin the first note.

Slur-Legato Etude

22

Semi-Staccato

The SEMI-STACCATO (Soft-Staccato, Half-Staccato) ( ) indicates that the notes must be only slightly separated with each note being softly articulated. This is also sometimes referred to as Legato tonguing. Most wind players associate this with the "du" attack.

Semi-Staccato Etude

Allegretto

Tenuto

A line placed over or under a note ( ) indicates TENUTO or STRESS, which means that the note is to be sustained for its full value with equal dynamic emphasis. The note is tongued in a normal manner. Tenuto marks are sometimes accompanied by slurs ( ). This indicates that the notes are to be played in a connected manner while sustained for their full value. All of the notes enclosed are to be played in one breath and are tongued very softly. This articulation is sometimes called LEGATO DETACHE', and it is generally construed that the notes are to be sustained longer than the Semi-Staccato.

Apply the following to the Bb (Major) Concert scale:

Tenuto Etude

Largo

Accents

The horizontal ACCENT (>) calls for the initial emphasis of the note followed by a diminution of sound. The vertical mark usually referred to as MARCATO (ʌ) indicates a heavy accent. All notes are slightly separated.

Apply the following to the B♭ (Major) Concert scale:

Accent Etude

Moderato

Dynamics

pp	p	mp	mf	f	ff
Pianissimo (Very soft)	Piano (Soft)	Mezzo Piano (Medium soft)	Mezzo Forte (Medium loud)	Forte (Loud)	Fortissimo (Very loud)

Slowly (Reverse dynamic levels on repeat)

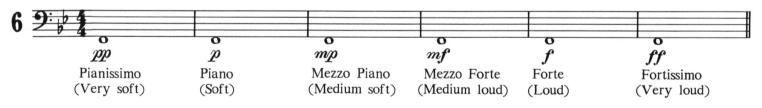

On the following harmonized scale observe the dynamic marks indicated or those dictated verbally by your director:

RHYTHM STUDIES

The ETUDES in <u>Unit X</u> contain most of the common rhythms found in musical literature. In addition, there is an ETUDE covering the complex problems of syncopation as well as $\frac{9}{8}$, $\frac{12}{8}$ and $\frac{5}{4}$ meters. Finally, an ETUDE containing mixed meters is presented as an aid in the preparation of much of today's contemporary music. Each ETUDE is preceded by a PREPARATORY DRILL. Repeat each measure of this drill until you are thoroughly familiar with the counting and the playing of the rhythm.

Eighths And Sixteenths In $\frac{2}{4}$ Time

Prep Drill

Etude

Moderato

Dotted Eighths And Sixteenths

Prep Drill

Etude

Allegretto

26

Syncopation*

Prep Drill

Etude

Moderato

Prep Drill

$\frac{9}{8}$ Time

Etude

Andantino

* Definition: A long note (or notes) between two short notes.

$\frac{12}{8}$ Time

Etude

Andante

$\frac{5}{4}$ Time

Prep Drill

Etude

Moderato

Mixed Meters

In much of the music of the Twentieth Century, composers are prone to changing time (meter) signatures quite often. You will probably not encounter as many changes as appear in the following etude. However, by mastering this study you will be better prepared for the performance of contemporary music.

Throughout most of the etude the beat (pulse) remains constant. New notes are assigned the value of the beat as indicated above the new signature. When you arrive at the $\frac{7}{8}$ time signature, however, there is actually a change in the pulse. The value of the eighth note is the same as the preceding measure, but the measure is limited to seven eighth-notes.

To better prepare for this situation practice the following Prep Drill. You will note that the value of the eighth note remains the same, but the meter change creates a change in the pulse. The cue notes under the basic notation will help you anticipate the change of pulse before arriving at the new time signature.

RUDIMENT REVIEW

A trained musician must not only be able to perform adequately on an instrument, but must also be able to communicate in the language of music. The material in <u>Unit XI</u> may be used as a review of your knowledge of the rudiments of music. Your teacher may use it as a test, or you may use it for self-evaluation. Become familiar with all of the material in <u>Unit XI</u> as well as the terms and symbols on the back inside cover. This will help you become a thorough musician.

1 Match the symbols with their names. For example, the first symbol is a bar line.

1. Measure	4. Natural	7. Double Bar
2. Sharp	5. Staff	8. Flat
3. Bar line	6. Bass Clef	9. Time Signature

Total points possible: 8

Your Score: _____

2 Match the notes with their names. For example, the first note is an Eighth Note.

1. Half Note	3. Quarter Note	5. Thirty-Second Note	7. Dotted Half Note
2. Dotted Eighth Note.	4. Whole Note	6. Sixteenth Note	8. Eighth Note

Total points possible: 7

Your Score:_____

3 Match the rests with their names. For example, the first rest is a Sixteenth Rest.

1. Eighth Rest	3. Thirty-Second Rest	5. Sixteenth Rest
2. Half Rest	4. Whole Rest	6. Quarter Rest

Total points possible: 5

Your Score:_____

4 Match the rests or rest patterns with their equivalent notations in $\frac{4}{4}$ time. For example, the first rest is the equivalent of an Eighth Note.

Total points possible: 8

Your Score: _____

5 Match the key signatures with the name of the key (major) indicated. For example, the first key signature indicates the key of Eb.

1. Bb	3. B	5. F	7. Eb	9. Db
2. A	4. D	6. G	8. Ab	

Total points possible: 8

Your Score: _____

6 Identify the following notes by placing the name in the square below.
For example, the first note is B♭.

```
Bb  ☐  ☐  ☐  ☐  ☐  ☐  ☐  ☐
```

Total points
possible: 9

Your Score:_____

7 Match the dynamic marking with its name. For example, the first dynamic marking
is called MEZZO FORTE.

1. Fortissimo (Very loud)
2. Mezzo Piano (Medium soft)
3. Forte (Loud)

4. Mezzo Forte (Medium loud)
5. Pianissimo (Very soft)
6. Piano (Soft)

mf   *mp*   *ff*   *f*   *p*   *pp*

4   ☐   ☐   ☐   ☐   ☐

Total points
possible: 5

Your Score: _____

8 A <u>Major Scale</u> is constructed with a series of whole steps and half steps as indicated below.
The <u>C Major Scale</u> is the only major scale that does not employ accidentals or a key signature.
Use this scale as a guide for constructing your own major scale.

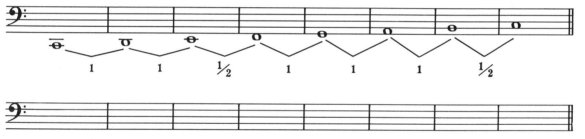

Starting on any note other than C construct a major scale. Be sure to
indicate the proper accidental(s).

Total points
possible for
correct scale: 8

Your Score: _____

9 A <u>Minor Scale</u> is constructed with a series of whole steps and half steps as indicated below. In
the <u>Harmonic Form</u> of the minor scale the 7th tone is raised a half step by means of an accidental
which does not appear in the key signature. The following <u>A Minor Scale</u> is the only minor scale
that does not employ a key signature.

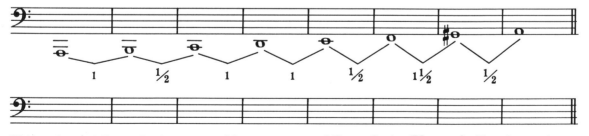

Using the <u>A Minor Scale</u> as a guide construct a Minor Scale (Harmonic Form) starting
on any note other than A. Be sure to indicate the proper accidental(s).

Total points
possible for
correct scale: 8

Your Score: _____

10 A musician must be able to recognize and 'hear' an interval in order to execute it properly on an instrument. One of the most common intervals is the MAJOR THIRD. This interval consists of two whole steps. Write in the correct note that will create the interval of a MAJOR THIRD. Be sure to supply accidentals where necessary.

MAJOR THIRD

Total points possible: 8

Your Score:_____

Another common interval is that of a PERFECT FOURTH. This interval consists of two whole steps and a half step. Write in the correct note that will create the interval of a PERFECT FOURTH. Be sure to supply accidentals where necessary.

PERFECT FOURTH

Total points possible: 8

Your Score:_____

Another common interval is that of a PERFECT FIFTH. This interval consists of three whole steps and a half step. Write in the correct note that will create the interval of a PERFECT FIFTH. Be sure to supply accidentals where necessary.

PERFECT FIFTH

Total points possible: 8

Your Score:_____

ENHARMONIC tones are those which sound the same and are fingered the same way but are written differently. For example, C♯ and D♭ actually sound the same and are fingered in the same way. Write in the enharmonic equivalent of the following notes. The first one has been done for you.

Total points possible: 8

Your Score:_____

Complete the following ascending and descending chromatic scales. Use sharps for the ascending scale and flats for the descending scale. Use only those accidentals that are necessary.

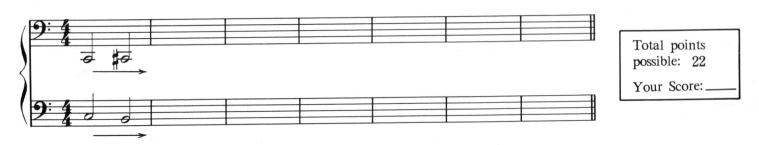

Total points possible: 22

Your Score:_____

TOTAL POINTS POSSIBLE IN UNIT XI: 120   YOUR SCORE:_____